HIDDEN
TREASURES

HIDDEN TREASURES

DAILY DEVOTIONALS

ALEIGHA C. ISRAEL

DEDICATED TO

MY WONDERFUL PARENTS.

I wouldn't have been able to write this book without you! For nineteen years (and counting), you've brought me up in the fear and admonition of the Lord; teaching me according to His Word. It was through your teachings and inspiration that I was encouraged to delve deeper into the understanding of the Bible.

You are my greatest blessings.
I love you, Mama and Daddy!

"Search for them as you
would for silver; seek them
like hidden treasures."
PROVERBS 2:4

ACKNOWLEDGMENTS

MY HEAVENLY FATHER: WITHOUT YOU, THIS book would have been nothing; I would have had nothing to write. Thank you for never giving up on me. Thank you for never leaving my side! I love you, Father!

Daddy and Mama: Thank you for all you've done for me and my books! I truly wouldn't have been able to do any of this without your help! There has never been a moment when I needed help and guidance and you weren't there. I love you!

My siblings: Y'all are the best! I can always count on you to tell me exactly what you think of my stories and ideas (and most of the time that *is* a good thing). You are a great encouragement to me!

My grandparents: I thank God that He chose to give me godly grandparents! You all are such a blessing to me. You encourage me to keep writing and using my gifts for God's glory. I love you all!

Aunt Leisha: Thank you for the wonderful cover! I can't even begin to describe how thankful I am that you are always so willing to design the covers for my books! You are such a blessing to me in many ways. Love you!

Emily: Thank you for making the map for *A Dim Reflection*! I was able to use it again in this book, and it still looks as wonderful as ever! You have an amazing gift. Keep using it for God's glory, and He will bless you abundantly!

Lindsay: Thanks for coming to my aid and helping me out with the formatting and interior design! Trying to do it myself this time only sealed the fact that I was meant to write the stories, not format them!

I truly couldn't do any of this without you!

Thank you so much!

My readers: An author can write a book, but without readers, it stays unread. It's because of you that I keep on writing! If you are reading this, thank you! And may you be blessed by the insights and stories that have blessed me.

TO MY READERS

I DON'T FEEL QUALIFIED TO WRITE THIS BOOK.

I struggle every day with trusting God and worrying about the future.

I often find myself struggling against being grumpy and not having a cheerful countenance.

I'm not perfect. I have my fair share of daily struggles, and it's because of that that I've written this book.

I haven't written this book because I *don't* struggle in these areas. I wrote it because I *do.*

Many times I find myself thinking back to the words I've written; usually I'm reminding myself that it's a sin to worry and be anxious about tomorrow.

But through my struggling, I've found answers that have helped me. I've found scriptures that are a great encouragement to me.

My prayer is that you too can find answers and relief from the daily struggles of life.

We search for answers, and peace, and relief from our suffering. But the answers have been right before our eyes the entire time!

They are in *God's Word.*

God's Holy Word can answer just about any question you have!

God's Word teaches us how to deal with anxiety, depression, pride, jealousy, and so much more!

I've found the answers to many of my struggles, and because of that, I want to share them with *you.*

But keep this in mind as you read this book; even though we might have found the answers, *only God can change our hearts.*

HIDDEN
TREASURES

We're traveling the path to the little white church. It's only a mile long, but the road is steep in certain places, making for a good workout.

The sun shines brightly, but the wind wins the battle this time.

I shove my hands in the pockets of my light jacket and pick up my pace.

Everything's quiet and peaceful. The journey to the church is always that way.

For forty or so minutes you can leave the world behind, and bask in the tranquility of God's creation.

No ringing telephones.

No noisy electronics.

No nagging alerts to check your e-mail or text messages.

It's simplicity at its best.

It's peaceful.

And other than personal Bible time, it's my favorite part of each day.

We top the hill, my sister's dog panting from the exertion.

Without fail, every time we walk past this hill, Woody is always here to greet us. Only Woody doesn't really care about us at all. Woody is only concerned about his prize, his treasure.

He's persistent, I'll give him that.

The hollow, *tap, tap tap,* never fails to bring a smile to my face.

Woody is a woodpecker.

He's just one of the wild creatures we've named on this route to the church. But Woody is by far, my favorite.

Why?

Well, because he's an inspiration. He's a reminder.

But before you're able to understand that statement, you'll need to know just a few woodpecker facts.

- ❖ The pileated woodpecker can strike a tree trunk at around 20 times per second.
- ❖ They strike the tree with the speed of 16 mph.
- ❖ They do this about 12,000 times a day, average.

Imagine you're a beautiful woodpecker.

You not only have to hunt for your food, but once you've found it you must dig a hole to get to it.

Now that you've finished that task you get to enjoy the quick snack. But then you're back to work and you do it all over again.

12,000 more times to be exact (give or take a few).

The woodpecker is a picture of persistence.

He doesn't stop at any cost. He pecks away with only one thought in mind: getting to his prize.

If only we could feel the same way about God's word.

If thou seekest her as silver, and searchest for her as for hidden treasures; Then shalt thou understand the fear of the Lord, and find the knowledge of God.
PROVERBS 2: 4-5

If only we could search for wisdom and understanding just as the woodpecker searches for his prize.

If you had reason to believe there was a treasure chest hidden in your backyard, would you sit still and do nothing?

Or would you take your finest shovels and digging equipment outside and begin searching at once?

Probably the latter.

So what should make God's Word any less valuable than the treasure in your backyard?

One of my favorite things to do is go *scripture hunting.* I'll flip through my Bible in search of scriptures that bring me joy and peace. When I find one, I'll underline it in a specific color.

If I'm feeling down or troubled all I have to do is flip through my Bible in search of scriptures underlined in florescent green.

So how can we search God's Word as hidden treasure?

Here are a few ideas:

- ❖ Read slowly; we can retain more that way.
- ❖ Try reading aloud.
- ❖ Ask the Lord for insight and understanding.

We come to know God and His wisdom when we search for it with our whole heart.

We find understanding when we seek it like silver and search for it like hidden treasure.

The Bible says if we seek it, we shall find it.

"Ask and it will be given to you; seek
and you will find; knock and the
door will be opened to you."
MATTHEW 7:7

Have a heart of understanding. A humble, broken spirit and a contrite heart. (Psalm 51:17)

Always be quick to listen and slow to speak.

There's a reason God gave us two ears and only one mouth!

We should never be afraid to ask God for help and insight when we don't understand something. He's perfectly capable of answering our many questions. He wants us to understand.

Pray for wisdom and understanding. Search for them as hidden treasures. And guess what? We'll find some, if we enlist His help.

Don't stop when you get tired.

Don't stop when it gets difficult.

And always remember this...the treasure is *always* worth the effort.

MOST
MISINTERPRETED
SENTENCE

This is a topic that has been on my mind for quite some time now. I can't say exactly why I haven't sat down to write the words that have been so heavy on my mind.

Perhaps because they need to be said in just the right way, in a way I still might not be able to put into words.

But as its popularity is beginning to grow, I can't seem to keep silent any longer.

Please remember as you read this though, that this is just an opinion. It's my opinion, but that doesn't mean it must be yours. And by no means am I saying this is the only right opinion. But, I'll continue and let you form your own on the matter.

"God answered my prayer!"

I do believe this is the most misused sentence I've yet to hear.

Or rather, "misinterpreted, and underrated," I should say. But let me explain.

The story below might give you an example of what I'm trying to relate.

Kara Evans is only six years old. But that doesn't stop her from wanting a little sibling more than anything else.

For the last year, (a very long time in a six-year old's mind, I should add) Kara has prayed and prayed for a baby brother or sister.

After many months of praying, Kara's mother and father told her they had a big surprise for her. She was going to be a big sister! Kara was ecstatic. The Lord had answered her prayers!

Kara had to wait a very long time for that sibling to be born. But she wasn't idle while she waited. During the time she was waiting for her sibling, she prayed with all her might that it would be a baby girl. She perhaps even prayed harder than she ever had before.

The day finally came when Kara's grandmother came to pick her up. That meant the baby would be here soon! Kara was so excited that night she could hardly sleep.

The next morning her grandmother handed her the phone. "It's your father, Kara. He's going to tell you if you have a baby brother or baby sister!" Kara held the phone to her ear and listened carefully as her father began to speak. It had to be a girl, it just had to be!

Kara's eyes grew wide with excitement as she hung up the phone and ran through the house yelling, "God answered my prayer! He answered my prayer!"

Now if I stopped right there and asked you what gender the baby was, what would you say? A girl, right? But what is the right answer?

A boy.

What? A boy? *But-but, Aleigha,* you might argue, *you just said the Lord had answered Kara's prayer!*

Yes. I did. And yes, He did answer Kara's prayer, just not in the way she'd prayed for it to be answered. Do you see where I'm going with this?

In my closet, there are two glass jars nestled amongst the books in one of the bookshelves. One jar holds prayers, and the other holds answered prayers.

Very soon after I'd picked up my "prayer jars," we received the news that a friend of ours was critically ill.

For many months, his health fluctuated from better to worse. And for many months, prayers for him poured forth from families everywhere.

Many slips of paper were dropped into that jar, and many hours were spent praying on his behalf.

We prayed for healing, peace, and mercy to be shown to this family. We prayed that this certain man might live for many more years with his family; and one night those prayers were answered.

He left his earthly home to join his Father and Creator in Heaven.

That was when I really started thinking about the saying, "God answered my prayer." I wonder why we are always so quick to think prayers must be answered in the way they've been asked.

Where do you think the prayers went that I'd written for this man? They went in the answered prayer jar.

I must admit though, it took a while before I got the courage to put them there. In my stubborn mind, those prayers were still unanswered.

But they *were* answered, just not exactly in the way I'd hoped they would be. But I'd received an answer nevertheless.

I once heard someone say that the Lord answers our prayers with one of three answers: *yes, no,* or *wait.* As time goes on, I'm beginning to see that to be true.

I don't believe there's anything wrong with saying the Lord answered your prayer. I think though, that it goes way deeper than just that. I believe the prayers that get a *no* or *wait* answer from God, get little to no attention sometimes. And if they *do* get attention, it's usually negative.

When was the last time we thanked God for *not* answering our prayers in the way we asked?

I know, it sounds crazy, believe me, I understand. But has there ever been a time when you've just thanked Him for answering a prayer according to *His* will?

We pray that ever familiar saying, "not my will, but Yours be done," but do we truly thank Him when He actually does it?

It's not too easy. It seems difficult, if not somewhat cruel, to thank God for taking a loved one's life, or thanking Him when things don't work out right. But sometimes saying "thank you" is another way of saying, "I trust You," or "I believe You know what's best."

For starters, begin thanking the Lord for the prayers that haven't been answered in the way you've asked. It may be hard at first, but it gets easier. And you never know, you might just find yourself thanking Him for every little thing that goes wrong in the day! We often can't see the bigger scope of things. We know that everything God allows is for our good in some way or another. We just often don't understand *why* it's happening.

We must remember that everything happens for a purpose and according to His will.

I remember several years ago, when we'd spent *all* day in the kitchen cooking down fresh tomatoes from our garden to make tomato paste.

We'd literally spent hours working hard to make sure it wouldn't scorch, and then we still had to can them afterwards.

That afternoon, several pints of tomato paste sat on the counter making all that hard work worth the effort.

The next morning though, we discovered that none of the jars had sealed. Not even one. We had to throw them all away, trying not to think about how much time and energy went into the failed product.

Needless to say, we were nothing short of discouraged. Very, very, discouraged.

But then I had a thought, which I then voiced to the others. Maybe there was something terribly wrong with the tomatoes and it would have made us very sick. Maybe this was the Lord's way of protecting us from that.

It was a silly thought, and that probably wasn't the case at all, but it made the outcome much easier to accept.

I didn't know it then, but without even thinking about it I was accepting the Lord's will for that situation by understanding it was done for a purpose.

So am I implying it's wrong to say that God answered your prayer? No, not at all. But the next time you pray and ask God for something, and your prayer isn't answered like you wanted it to be, take a moment and thank Him anyway, because He *did* in truth, answer your prayer, just not in the way you intended.

So just try something the next time you run into another discouraging situation; try not only thanking Him, but try to remember He did it for a purpose.

And in the end, He did it for you. And He did it to prosper you, and to give you a future and a hope.

THE FINAL COUNTDOWN

After weeks of planning (and a lot of unnecessary fretting) the big day is finally here! You've worked hours and hours, slaving over plans, making sure every detail is in perfect order for the big day.

It could be a Christmas party, or a 4th of July cookout. Maybe it's a bridal shower, a birthday party or graduation ceremony. Whatever the event, you've worked hard for this day and tried to tone down the anxiety you feel about the upcoming party.

What if little Billy doesn't get along happily with the other boys?

What if Mrs. Jones forgets to bring the cutlery again?

What if Mr. Smith talks nonstop about that golfing tournament he won years ago, you know, the one he's told almost a hundred times now?

But as the day wears on, you begin to laugh quietly at your concern. *"It was all for nothing,"* you say.

Billy played happily with his friends.

Mrs. Jones remembered to bring the cutlery.

And miracles do happen, Mr. Smith didn't talk about his golfing tournament once!

Sound familiar?

Chances are, it does; because it's happened to all of us at one time or another.

But we know it's wrong to worry. And brace yourself for this; if we are anxious about something, we are actually sinning!

When we worry about something, we're failing to trust God and His goodness and refusing to believe what He's told us through His Word.

He commands us not to worry:

"Therefore I tell you, do not worry about your life, what you will eat or drink; or about your body, what you will wear. Is not life more than food, and the body more than clothes?"
MATTHEW 6:25

"Cast your cares on the Lord and He will sustain you; He will never let the right-eous be shaken."
PSALM 55:22

There are other verses. Many, many more verses that tell us not to worry.

Here are a few more dealing with this topic:

"Humble yourselves, therefore, under God's mighty hand, that He may lift you up in due time. Cast all your anxiety on Him because He cares for you."
1 PETER 5: 6-7

"Therefore, do not worry about tomorrow, for tomorrow will worry
about itself. Each day has enough
trouble of its own."
MATTHEW 6:34

"Do not be anxious about anything, but
in every situation, by prayer and peti-
tion, with thanksgiving, present your
requests to God. And the peace of God,
which transcends all understanding,
will guard your hearts and your minds
in Christ Jesus."
PHILIPPIANS 4:6-7

When we worry, it's easier for us to
be led astray and for Satan to get a foothold
in our lives.

We must trust in the Lord and
acknowledge that His plans are best.

"For I know the plans I have for you," declares the LORD, "plans to prosper you and not to harm you, plans to give you hope and a future."
JEREMIAH 29:11

I don't do well with uncertainty. I like to be in control and plan everything days ahead.

I'm the kind of person who would pack my suitcase weeks before the trip, (if I didn't need the stuff before leaving!)

So what gives me the strength to journey on?

What gives me the peace to live life joyfully day unto day?

What gives me the hope that whatever happens today or tomorrow, everything will work out fine?

That scripture you just read is the answer.

Who knows our plans?
God does.
Who makes our plans?
God does.
And what will those plans do?

They will give us hope, and a future.

Now I'm not saying everything that happens to us will be all happy and perfect.

I know plenty of families right now who are struggling every day with the fact they might not have a family member with them in the following months.

They're going through a lot of uncertainty right now.

But I know without doubt, what keeps each of these families with the spirit and attitude they have every day.

They know who holds the future. And they're content to let Him guide them through each hour and take their burdens upon Himself.

They find rest in God, who desires to hold our burdens.

"Come to Me, all you who labor and are heavy laden, and I will give you rest. Take My yoke upon you and learn from Me, for I am gentle and lowly in heart, and you will find rest for your souls. For My yoke is easy and My burden is light."
MATTHEW 11:28-30

I've decided the future just isn't worth worrying over.

What will worrying do?

Nothing. Absolutely nothing. Not. One. Thing. It won't and can't change anything.

Is that to say I don't worry about anything? No. I still worry, a good bit more than I should. But when I start to worry, I just have to reflect upon the words I just wrote, and upon the fact God has said in His Word not to worry.

Are you worrying about something in your life right now? If so, take it to the Lord. Please, give it to Him. I've found it works much better that way.

He wants to carry our burdens on His shoulders (Psalm 55:22, Matthew 11:28). Shoulders that are much more capable and stronger than ours.

Give everything to Him and trust Him fully.

He alone will give you the strength and peace to journey on.

FEAR

fear

/ˈfir/

noun
an unpleasant emotion caused by the belief that someone or something is dangerous, likely to cause
pain, or a threat.

FALSE

EVIDENCE

APPEARING

REAL

Fear is lurking all around us. It's hiding in the most imperceptible places and trying its best to get a foothold in our minds.

And those of us who have given in to fear, know without a doubt the power it has in slowly destroying our lives.

Would you believe me if I told you fear can be a good thing?

Now, I'm not talking about the kind of fear you experience when you're late for work, dreading the interaction with your boss. Or the fear of thunder storms, bugs, or other phobias.

I'm not talking about the fear that's evoked from an abusive spouse, or parent.

I'm not talking about the fear of *man*. I'm talking about the fear of *God*.

Throughout the Bible we are told to fear God. But what does that mean?

R.C. Sproul answers that question quite nicely in the following words: *"We need to make some important distinctions about the biblical meaning of "fearing" God. These distinctions can be helpful, but they can also be a little dangerous. When Luther struggled with that, he made this distinction, which has since become somewhat famous: He distinguished between what he called a servile fear and a filial fear.*

The servile fear is a kind of fear that a prisoner in a torture chamber has for his tormentor, the jailer, or the executioner. It's that kind of dreadful anxiety in which someone is frightened by the clear and present danger that is represented by another person. Or it's the kind of fear that a slave would have at the hands of a malicious mas-

ter who would come with the whip and torment the slave. Servile refers to a posture
of servitude toward a malevolent owner.

Luther distinguished between that
and what he called filial fear, drawing from
the Latin concept from which we get the
idea of family. It refers to the fear that a
child has for his father. In this regard, Luther is thinking of a child who has tremen-
dous respect and love for his father or
mother and who dearly wants to please
them. He has a fear or an anxiety of offend-
ing the one he loves, not because he's afraid
of torture or even of punishment, but rather because he's afraid of displeasing the
one who is, in that child's world, the source
of security and love.

I think this distinction is helpful because the basic meaning of fearing the Lord
that we read about in Deuteronomy is also
in the Wisdom Literature, where we're told
that "the fear of the Lord is the beginning
of wisdom." The focus here is on a sense of
awe and respect for the majesty of God.
That's often lacking in contemporary evan-
gelical Christianity. We get very flippant

and cavalier with God, as if we had a causal relationship with the Father. We are invited to call him Abba, Father, and to have the personal intimacy promised to us, but still we're not to be flippant with God. We're always to maintain a healthy respect and adoration for him.

One last point: If we really have a healthy adoration for God, we still should have an element of the knowledge that God can be frightening. "It is a frightening thing to fall into the hands of the living God" (Heb. 10:31). As sinful people, we have every reason to fear God's judgment; it is part of our motivation to be reconciled with God."

From those two commentaries, and from studying the Bible ourselves, what are some ways we can understand the fear of God? And how can we make sure we are fearing Him?

❖ Read Proverbs 2
❖ Learn from Jesus Christ who feared His Father with perfect fear

To understand the fear of God, we must:

- ❖ Receive correction and advice
- ❖ Listen for wisdom and understanding
- ❖ Yearn for discernment and understanding
- ❖ Treasure these things within you

*"...If you look for it as for silver
and search for it as for hidden treasure,
then you will understand the fear of the
Lord and find the knowledge of God. For
the Lord gives wisdom; from His mouth
come knowledge and understanding. He
holds success in store for the upright..."*
PROVERBS 2:4-7

If we fear the Lord, then He will:

- ❖ Be a shield to us
- ❖ Guard our path
- ❖ Preserve our way
- ❖ Deliver us from evil and from men who speak perverse things
- ❖ Deliver us from immoral women

And:

- ❖ We will understand righteousness and justice, equity and every good path
- ❖ Discretion will preserve us
- ❖ Understanding will keep us
- ❖ We will walk in the way of goodness
- ❖ We will keep to the path of the righteous

Child-like fear of God will:

- ❖ Restrain us from sin
- ❖ Foster integrity
- ❖ Promote obedience to His commandments
- ❖ Magnify our love for God
- ❖ Work covenant loyalty
- ❖ Trump slavish fear of man
- ❖ Promote a healthy respect
- ❖ Produce a zeal for evangelism
- ❖ Bring us all kinds of blessings: goodness, family security, wisdom, and happiness

The fear of God is a topic that stretches far beyond the pages of this book.

The amount of knowledge one can learn concerning it, is much greater than what I've written.

In fact, I once attended a conference where the main theme was learning about the fear of God.

The conference was even titled, *The Fear of God,* and many of my notes are within the pages you just read.

Many thanks go to all the speakers who shared with us during those few days, specifically *Dr. Joel Beeke, Dr. Carlton McLeod, and Sam Waldron.* Their teachings inspired me to dig deeper into understanding the true meaning of the fear of God.

And my prayer is that you, dear reader, will do that as well.

Don't stop with the mere taste I've given you. Dig deeper and don't stop until you're able to completely and utterly give an answer to the question, *"what does it mean to fear God?"*

HE'S WATCHING YOU

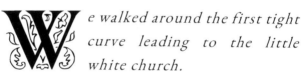**W**e walked around the first tight curve leading to the little white church.

My sister and I have been walking this road for quite some time now.

It's 10:00 am, but the road is never that busy.

The trees are shading the road and the brisk wind rattles the leaves, letting out a persistent howl.

Our giant Great Pyrenees sulks between us, her head hanging low. Her ears perk up as a dog's bark echoes in the distance.

I turn to my younger sister, my voice low. "Do you ever get the feeling we're being watched?"

She glances over her shoulder briefly and takes a minute before answering, her eyes widening slightly. "Um, sometimes, but not right now."

I smile mischievously. "Well, we should." I glance in her direction. "We're being watched every second of the day."

It's true, you know. *God is always watching us.*

That saying is so over used that we seem to drum it into the category of "cliché" and choose to forget all about it.

How many times in a day do we think to ourselves, "God is watching me"?

My answer would be, "not enough."

Before you speak harshly to your son or daughter, remember, *someone's watching you.*

Before you get angry with your spouse, remember, *someone's watching you.*

Before you reply impatiently to your sibling, remember, *someone's watching you.*

Before you choose to pursue a bad option on the internet, remember, *someone's watching you.*

And sometimes that *someone* might be someone else besides God.

Rest assured He's *always* watching us. But, we might have another pair of eyes observing our every move. A child. A spouse. A sibling.

An unbeliever.

That latter one should be enough to cause an earthquake in our souls. It should be enough to ensure that we're always on our best behavior.

Why?

Because what sin is more despicable than throwing aside God's commandments and making His name look filthy? I can think of a few, but that one alone is pretty bad.

How does one manage this, you might ask.

We are called to be "lights for Christ." A light in a world filled with darkness.

How obvious is a light in a dark room?

If we call ourselves lights, yet we do not shine, how hypocritical is that?

Not only hypocritical (and sinful), but obvious. Painfully obvious.

Which brings me to why I said what I did about unbelievers.

If we call ourselves Christians, yet don't act like it, we are giving a bad name for Christ.

If I call myself a Christian, yet speak impatiently, it only gives an unbeliever a reason to say, "Well, look at her, she calls herself a Christian yet speaks the same way I do."

It's impossible to act perfectly every second of the day. Believe me, I know. I'm far from perfect. But we must keep our lights shining. If we call ourselves Christians, we must be a light to those around us.

How do we do that? What's the formula for being *lights for Christ?*

Here are a few helpful tips that have helped me out along the way:

THE RECIPE:

INGREDIENTS:

- ❖ 1 cup of *love*
- ❖ ½ cup of *patience*
- ❖ ½ cup of *kindness*
- ❖ ½ cup of *faith*
- ❖ 1 pinch of *1 Peter 3:15*
- ❖ 1 pound of *smiles*
- ❖ A dash of *joy, hope,* and *peace*

Method:

Blend everything together. Use immediately!

The reason I put a pound of smiles, is because I believe in the power of a happy countenance.

Have you ever stood back in a store and observed the people before you?

How many of them have a smile on their face? If you found five people, then send me a picture! I'd love to see the sight.

I've never counted more than two or three in my days of "people watching."

But you know what? Every time I smile at someone passing by, they smile right back. It's contagious! And guess what, you started it! Your smile was the cause of theirs. And your smile may have been just the thing they needed that day.

So, try something the next time you're out. Try smiling at ten different people. Watch and be amazed as their frown will most likely be turned upside down!

And remember, someone's *always* watching us! So let's make sure we're giving Christ a good name, and do our best to be lights for Him.

COUNTENANCE

There are some people
Who rush through their day,
Through breakfast and dinner
And lunch all the way.
They worry about things
That you shouldn't worry about,
They frown all the time
They shout and they pout.
But there is one thing
About that frown,
If you could turn it upside down,
Then a smile it would be.
How happy that would make
Both you and me!
So just try a little test
The next time you're around,
A frowny person
Try to turn their frown upside down!
And here's a little hint
Before you take the test,
Just wear a smile yourself
And try to do your best!

WHY WAIT?

recently attended the funeral of a 93-year-old woman who I only had the pleasure of meeting a few times before her death.

Her service was well attended, her obituary stirring—giving me a glimpse into her life.

She sounded like a wonderful person, leaving me to consider that if people had a third of the number of things to say about me at *my* funeral, I would have done pretty well in life.

But I left that day with a question on my mind.

Why wait?

Why do we wait until *after* the death of a loved one to write such touching tributes? Why do we wait until *after* they're gone to tell everyone how much they meant to us? Why do we wait to write and boast about them when they aren't even hearing the touching words we've written?

Well, for starters, it's culture. For as long as you and I can remember, it's always been this way.

Am I suggesting we change that? No, I'm not. Don't worry, I'm not about to start some "ban the obituary" pact. If it weren't for the beautiful tributes given by sons, daughters, grandchildren, and other relatives, I wouldn't have known much about this lady.

I think writing down your favorite memories and things about the deceased is a wonderful thing to do, not only in memory of the person, but also for family and friends attending the service.

We don't have to wait until our loved ones die to tell them how much they mean to us. We don't have to wait until they're gone to tell other people our favorite memories made with them. We don't have to wait another day to tell that sibling, father, mother, spouse, grandfather or grandmother how much their life means to us.

Am I telling you to write the obituary early? No, that would be just a little bizarre. But what you *can* do is make it a point to tell this certain person how much they mean to you.

You've probably heard the saying, "you don't realize what you have until it's gone." Chances are, you've heard sayings like that before and it's because they're so true.

You didn't realize how much you relied on that car, until the transmission broke and you had to take it to the shop.

You never thought about how much time that food processor was saving you until it broke in the middle of canning season.

You never stopped to think twice about how much you were relying on a loved one until you woke up one morning to find that they're gone.

That's hard to think about and even harder to comprehend. But statistics show that 151,600 people die every 24 hours. That's 6,316 people in an hour, 105 in every minute and nearly 2 people in every second of the day.

Death rate is one per person and you never know when you or a loved one will be next.

That's a sobering thought, but it's a necessary one.

So, what should you do now? I'd suggest taking the time to write a note to someone special in your life, telling them how much you love them.

Is it too hard to come up with something? Try closing your eyes for a minute and imagining they're gone.

What do you miss most about them? Write it down.

Do they make you smile? If so, how?

Do you have a favorite memory made with the person? Write it down.

And try to remember that life fades fast. In the blink of an eye, ten years will be gone, leaving you standing there wondering what just happened.

We should take every opportunity given to us and use it to tell others how much we love them. They won't be on this earth forever, and neither will we.

We should take advantage of who the Lord has blessed us with. One day we might wake up to find that they are no longer here.

We must live each day as if it's our last, and remember this: our Heavenly Father shows unconditional love towards us, so let's remember to share a little of that with others.

HOMEWORK:

Write a note to a loved one telling them how much they mean to you.

THINGS TO ASK YOURSELF:

❖ What do they do that makes you smile?

❖ What is your favorite memory with them?

❖ What gift(s) has God blessed them with?

This is also a good exercise to do if you're having a hard time being thankful for a certain person.

Are you having trouble keeping your children or siblings from quarreling? Write down the questions above and have them answer each one accordingly. You'll be amazed at the outcome!

THE HSW
METHOD

THE HSW METHOD

HEAR IT, SEE IT, AND WRITE IT!

Did you know that when you memorize a song, it makes the words really hard to forget?

We have gone once a month for several years to an assisted living home, playing music and singing for the residents. You would be surprised at how many of those sweet residents still remember the words and tunes to so many of the songs that we sing.

Hearing the scriptures put to music is a key ingredient to easy memorizing.

So, upon that note, (no pun intended) let's get started!

HEAR IT:
Put music to the scriptures.

Take the verses that you would like to memorize and try putting music to them. It can be music from a song that you like or a completely made-up tune. It also helps if you split the verse into sections. I have put an example below:

I CORINTHIANS 13:4

- ❖ Love suffers long and is kind
- ❖ Love does not envy
- ❖ Love does not parade itself
- ❖ Is not puffed up

Memorize each section of the verse and then add on another section. Before you know it, you will have the entire verse memorized!

SEE IT:
Take your verse and read it.

Over and over and over again. Read it using a strong inflection upon a different word each time. Put an exaggerated inflection on each bold word below:

❖ **Love** suffers long and is kind, love does not envy, love does not parade itself, is not puffed up.

❖ Love **suffers** long and is kind, love does not envy, love does not parade itself, is not puffed up.

❖ Love suffers **long** and is kind, love does not envy, love does not parade itself, is not puffed up.

❖ Love suffers long **and** is kind, love does not envy, love does not parade itself, is not puffed up.

Keep doing that until all the words have been used up. You will be amazed at how different it sounds too! You might even learn something new by reading it that way.

Do that a few times until you are ready to move on.

WRITE IT:

Get a piece of paper and copy your verse. Copy it at least five times. After that, you should be able to write it almost without looking.

Remember, don't get discouraged, and have fun! Memorizing God's word is not only a fun thing to do, but it is also commanded:

"This Book of the Law shall not depart from your mouth, but you shall meditate in it day and night, that you may observe to do according to all that is written in it. For then you will make your way prosperous, and then you will have good success."
JOSHUA 1:8

"Let the word of Christ dwell in you richly in all wisdom, teaching and admonishing one another in psalms and hymns and spiritual songs, singing with grace in your hearts to the Lord.
COLOSSIANS 3:16

"I have not departed from the commandment of His lips; I have treasured the words of His mouth more than my necessary food."
JOB 23:12

Memorize as many scriptures as you can. Believe me, they will soon come in handy!

NOTES:

❖ It's important to memorize only one verse at a time. Once you have it down, then add another verse, saying both verse one and verse two, one after the other.

❖ You may find it necessary to use only one part (Hear It, See It, or Write It) to memorize a scripture. For example, I can put a tune to the scripture and read it a few times, without having to write it down. Just play with it and see what works best for you.

❖ Remember, have fun and take joy in hiding God's Word in your heart!

TRAVELING
ON

The sun shines brightly upon the road, illuminating the path before us.

We step off the asphalt and onto the grass, waving at the car passing by.

We top the first hill, stopping a moment to let our dog catch her breath... Yes, I did just say dog.

I'm convinced we own the laziest dog on the planet.

Okay, maybe that's a bit too harsh of an accusation. She is a Great Pyrenees, and she is a nocturnal animal. So, dragging her along with us on our walks to the church, in her mind, is a ridiculous act of trickery.

I guess I wouldn't appreciate it if someone woke me up in the middle of the night, and forced me to go on a walk.

My sister gives a quick tug to the leash and encourages her to go further. "Come on, Gracie, you can do it!"

Gracie's ears perk up at the sound of her name, and her tail wags a little faster.

She picks up her pace slightly and continues on. That is, until she tires again, which is usually only after a couple minutes.

"We're almost there, Gracie!" "You can do it!" "Come on, girl."

Our encouragement seems to fall on deaf ears as she slows her pace.

I glance around me, laughing silently. If only the neighbors saw us now, encouraging a dog to walk two miles.

With a little more encouragement and the mention that the waterfall is not too far away, she picks up her pace once again.

Mentioning the waterfall always does the trick. The only problem is, we never go there. It's too secluded.

We finally arrive at the little white church, Gracie panting between us.

She glances towards the path leading to the waterfall and looks up at us with hopeful eyes.

"Sorry girl, not this time." Or in other words, "not ever."

We turn around at the end of the road and begin the trek back to the house.

Gracie's energy seems to evaporate once she understands we aren't headed to the waterfall.

Our words of encouragement start again as Gracie sulks between us. "Come on girl, we're almost home!"

You see, Gracie never thinks she can make the journey to the church and back. Yet every time, without fail, she does.

She thinks she's too tired.

She thinks she's too hot.

She wishes the end destination were different.

But Gracie always makes it.

Is there a *Gracie* in your life? Do you have a loved one who is discouraged; who doesn't ever think they have what it takes to travel on?

Are you the encourager in their life, or do you want to be, but you don't know how?

Gracie's a dog, as we all know by now, but she reminds me of a discouraged individual who lives their lives in the slums of depression.

An individual who always wishes she were somewhere else, doing something else, being with someone else. Maybe they wish they were someone else entirely.

Depression and discontentment. They are two completely different things, yet they feed off each other.

Depression affects more than 15 million American adults, or about 6.7 percent of the U.S. population age 18 and older in a given year.

It's debilitating, it's frustrating, and you want it to stop.

Discontentment is the same way, yet you can usually find a reason for your feelings.

What does the Bible say about discontentment?

Well, for starters, it's sin.

But how do we define discontentment? And how do we *stop* being discontent?

First, let's look at the definition of discontentment:

DISCONTENT: Relentless desire for something different.

So, in other words, we always wish things were different than how they are. We're never content with what we have.

We're always looking for that next big adventure, never being satisfied with what we have here and now.

Never having enough.

Discontentment is disobedience towards God.

Apparently, the apostle Paul had a hard time with discontentment. Only by reading chapter 4 of Philippians, do we read that he "learned the secret" of being content in every circumstance.

What's the secret? We see the answer in Philippians 4:13. *I can do all things through Him who gives me strength.*

Some people interpret that verse as meaning they can accomplish literally anything their minds can perceive.

Paul's words, when properly understood, are far more expansive than that interpretation of the verse: Because of Christ, we can accomplish contentment no matter what circumstances a day brings into our lives.

Why is contentment so important?

It's important to first realize how sinful our discontentment really is. Founder's Ministries does a great job at listing some of the ways we let discontentment infest itself in our lives. Here are a few that I've paraphrased:

❖ **Discontentment is not trusting in God.** Contentment is trusting God completely. So naturally, discontentment is the opposite.

❖ **Discontentment is complaining against God's plan.** We think our desires and plans are better than God's.

❖ **Discontentment displays a desire to be sovereign.** Like Adam and Eve, we desire to taste of the tree that will transform us into "something better."

❖ **Discontentment covets something God has not been pleased to give us.** He gave us His Son; therefore, can we not trust Him for the trivial things? (Rom. 8:32)

❖ **Discontentment subtly (or perhaps not so subtly) communicates that God has made a mistake.** It's thinking that our present circumstances are wrong and they should be otherwise. We will only be content when they change to fit our desires.

❖ **Discontentment denies the wisdom of God and exalts my wisdom.** Isn't this precisely what Eve did in the garden in questioning the goodness of God's Word? Thus, discontentment was at the heart of the first sin. "Has God really said?" That's the question at the heart of all our discontentment.

So now that we've defined what it means to be *discontent.* How do we make sure our lives are filled with *contentment?*

Founder's Ministries lists 6 Battle-Tested Ways to Becoming More Content:

❖ **Conditions and circumstances in life are always changing, therefore my satisfaction and joy must not be tied to circumstances.** Jesus must not be one who merely meets our material and physical needs. Jesus is not a divine ATM. John Piper's words are sobering and penetrating here: "I'll tell you what makes Jesus look beautiful. It's when you smash your car and your little child smashes through the windshield and lands dead on the street, and you say, through the deepest possible pain, 'God is enough. He is good. He will take care of us. He will satisfy us. He will see us through this. He is our treasure.' Whom have I in heaven but you and on earth there is nothing that I desire besides you, my flesh and my heart and my little child may fail, but you are the strength of my heart and my portion forever. That makes God look glorious as God, not as giver of cars or safety or health.... God is most glorified in us when we are most satisfied in Him in the midst of loss, not prosperity." Thus, contentment comes when I melt my will and my desires into Christ's will and desires, even when I struggle to understand my circumstances.

❖ **What matters supremely in life is my soul and my relationship to God.** Christ's death and resurrection is my only hope. Hope may be our most powerful possession. Hope is the sunshine and rain of our life—it is what makes us grow and thrive. Without it, we won't flourish. An old saying applies here: "Human beings can live 40 days without food, four days without water, and four minutes without air, but we can't live four seconds without hope." And we have a sure and settled hope as the anchor of our souls *(Heb. 6:19)*.

❖ **God is concerned about me as my Father, and nothing happens to me apart from His will.** Even the hairs on my head are numbered. He is meticulously sovereign. He is good and He delights to give good gifts to His children *(Matt. 7:7–11)*.

❖ **God's will and God's ways are a great mystery, but I know that whatever he wills or permits is for my good.** Every situation in life is an unfolding of some manifestation of God's love and goodness. Therefore, my business is to look for each special manifestation of God's goodness and be prepared for surprises and blessings. Romans 8:28 is not a trite cliché, but a glorious promise for God's children that serves as solid ground for their feet.

❖ **I must not regard my circumstances and conditions in and of themselves, but as part of God's dealings with me** in the work of perfecting my soul and bringing me to final perfection. In a life east of Eden, suffering will be a major part of this. We must burn into our minds and hearts the words of the psalmist in 145:17, "The Lord is righteous in all his ways and kind in all his works."

❖ Whatever my condition may be at this present moment, it is only temporary, it is passing, and can never rob me of the joy and the glory that ultimately await me in Christ. To be content, I must realize that my inheritance is in heaven and it is being guarded to be revealed on the last day *(1 Peter 1:4)*. Paul called his affliction momentary and light *(2 Cor. 4:16–18)*, even though he suffered in ways the vast majority of us never will. See his ministry resume in 2 Cor. 11:16–29 for a stunning laundry list of Paul's sufferings in service of the gospel.

If you're struggling with discontentment in your life, take it to Jesus. Pray faithfully that He will take away your heart of unhappiness and put in its place a heart of thankfulness.

Do you have a *Gracie* in your life who needs to hear this?

Share it with them and pray for them daily.

And remember this: you can talk with them and pray for them, but only God can change a heart.

GOOD
ENOUGH

"It's good enough."

How many times do we, as Christians, utter that phrase? We tackle a task, only to say towards the end, "that's good enough."

But good enough for what? And good enough for whom?

If a football player is required to do warmups for 20 minutes, and he only does 15 (because he gets tired) and declares, "that's good enough," is it really?

Good enough for what? And good enough for whom?

This morning I made my bed as usual. (If there's one thing I *used* to have OCD about, it's my bed.)

I had strict instructions and goals when making my bed. The comforter hangs over the bed only so much. The pillows *must* be fluffed (and there are six of them); you get the picture.

I've instilled this OCD in my 8-year-old sister. That's probably part of the reason why I don't have it anymore.

In fact, she's the one who brought to my attention this morning that the comforter wasn't hanging *perfectly* straight over the side of the bed. And because I didn't feel like fixing it, what was my response? You guessed it. *"It's good enough."*

Which got me thinking. Good enough for what? And good enough for whom?

Who do we make our beds for? Who do we cook our meals for? Who do we do the laundry for?

The answer's not *me,* or *us.* It's not our *husbands,* or our *families.*

The answer is *Christ.*

We work for Christ.

We play for Christ.

We do *everything* for Christ.

We don't (or shouldn't) do things to receive praise from man. We should do everything with only one figure in mind, *Christ.*

Those aren't my words either. Take a look at this verse in Ephesians:

"Serve wholeheartedly, as if you were serving the Lord, not people,"
EPHESIANS 6:7

And a few more speaking on this topic:

"Whatever you do, work at it with all your heart, as working for the Lord, not for human masters."
COLOSSIANS 3:23

"So whether you eat or drink or whatever you do, do it all for the glory of God."
1 CORINTHIANS 10:31

This one right here is humbling:

"Am I now trying to win the approval of human beings, or of God? Or am I trying to please people? If I were still trying to please people, **I would not be a servant of Christ**."
GALATIANS 1:10

Paul tells us in his letter to the Galatians, that if we are serving man rather than God, we aren't servants of Christ.

I don't know about you, but I would never want to fall under that category!

How do we make certain that we aren't serving man rather than God? And if we are, how do we stop it?

Do we even know the difference?

How do we know for sure if we are serving man rather than Christ?

Well, for starters, serving the Lord means we are not serving ourselves.

Serving the Lord means we are not *primarily* serving others.

Don't get me wrong, serving others is definitely not a sin, in fact we are commanded to serve others:

"You, my brothers and sisters, were called to be free. But do not use your freedom to indulge the flesh; rather, serve one another humbly in love."
GALATIANS 5:13

"Each of you should use whatever gift you have received to serve others, as faithful stewards of God's grace in its various forms."
1 PETER 4:10

"Love must be sincere. Hate what is evil; cling to what is good. Be devoted to one another in love. Honor one another above yourselves. Never be lacking in zeal, but keep your spiritual fervor, serving the Lord. Be joyful in hope, patient in affliction, faithful in prayer. Share with the Lord's people who are in need. Practice hospitality."
ROMANS 12: 9-13

In fact, when we're serving others, we *are* serving God!

"The King will reply, 'Truly I tell you, whatever you did for one of the least of these brothers and sisters of mine, you did for me.'"
MATTHEW 25:40

What brings us pleasure? How do we please ourselves?

It could be ice cream, movies, food, shopping, reading, the possibilities are endless.

These are some of the ways we serve ourselves rather than God.

Am I implying that it's wrong to shop? Wrong to eat? Wrong to watch movies?

No, we would die if we didn't eat, and we should definitely wear clothes!

What I am saying is this: Enjoying a bowl of ice cream is not necessarily wrong (unless we're being gluttons, which in that case, it's sin) but often, we aren't serving Christ while doing so.

Imagine yourself with a mop in one hand, and a mop bucket in the other (for some people, this may be difficult).

Now imagine yourself mopping a floor and doing the best job you've ever done before.

Why are you doing this? Because your boss is going to be looking over it later.

You stand back and admire your work.

The floor shines so brightly you almost have to look away.

It looks better than it ever has, if you do say so yourself.

Then your supervisor comes to look it over.

Maybe it's your father, maybe it's your mother, maybe it's a sibling, or a boss. Whoever it may be, you've been waiting for this moment with great expectation.

What are you waiting for?

Praise. Adoration. Encouragement. After receiving it, you go happily on your way, rejoicing in another task well done.

But let's rewind for a minute, back to where we were before the supervisor came to look over your work.

Let's say he comes, but he doesn't offer you any praise, adoration or encouragement.

Let's imagine he doesn't say anything at all.

He glances at your work, gives a half nod of approval and goes on his way.

How does that make you feel?

Broken.

Discouraged.

Upset.

Unappreciated.

Why would his reaction have such an effect on you?

Because you were mopping the floor for *him.*

You were working for him, you were serving him, and when you didn't get the reaction you'd expected, you became discouraged.

You see, if you would have mopped the floor for Christ, doing your best, not expecting praise, or anything else in return, you would have had no reason to grow discouraged because of your overseer's reaction.

Children could win the prize at being the best man pleasers in the world.

They do things to please their parents and they blossom under praise and encouragement. It's a part of who they are.

But as they grow older, they must be taught they aren't doing these things to please their parents, but they are doing it to please the Lord.

And when children do things to please the Lord, it also pleases their parents!

Even the best, most sacrificial things (if done to please men) are worth nothing in God's eyes.

I love to give gifts. I love seeing the smile spread over a little child's face, or the joy on an adult's.

Gift-giving is contagious, and I can truthfully say I love giving gifts much more than I enjoy receiving them.

But I didn't use to have such a good attitude about giving gifts. In fact, I used to give gifts to please man, rather than God.

An exciting idea formed when I was around twelve-years-old.

I wanted to collect Bibles to give to people in need.

I started out using my own money, but the Lord soon blessed me by other family members and friends who mailed Bibles and sent money.

I was ecstatic!

Many times, as a child, our Thanksgivings would be spent serving the homeless in our community.

It was something we all looked forward to with great excitement.

It was such fun to serve others and enjoy the feeling of purpose.

It was around Thanksgiving when I first had the chance to give out some of these Bibles.

The gym was set up with tables to serve the homeless a hot Thanksgiving meal, and we had many volunteers.

Timidly, I approached a table and handed a lady a Bible.

My mother, not very far behind me, became my spokeswoman, and talked with the lady for a few minutes while I listened.

Giving away Bibles became a favorite thing to do, and I found homes for every Bible that came into my possession.

Family members and friends were quick to offer encouragement and praise, and I soaked it all in.

It wasn't until a few months later, that I discovered something was wrong.

Something wasn't right. I didn't feel like I did when I first started giving away Bibles.

And then I noticed something else. The praise I had gotten from friends and family members had slowly waned, and with it, went my joyful desire to give away those Bibles.

That was when I realized something else.

My Bible giving days may have started out with an innocent motive. But I had let the praise of man enter my heart and turn my motives around. I had slowly, but surely, become a man pleaser.

So, I stopped giving away Bibles.

Why? Because my motive was all wrong. And until I could fix it, I decided to stop giving away Bibles.

That may not have been the wisest decision, but as a twelve-year-old, it was the best one I could think of.

Since then, I've learned that giving gifts for God's glory, reaps a much better reward than giving them to receive praise from man.

Just as working for Christ, and working to serve Him, rather than man, is not only Biblical, but it also makes us feel better in the process.

(Oh, and we've also went back to giving away Bibles, in bags we put together for the homeless!)

Are we serving man, rather than God?

If the answer is "yes," then we must ask the Lord's forgiveness and endeavor to change our perspective.

Here are a few tips to help in that process:

- ❖ Be quick to help others
- ❖ Practice hospitality
- ❖ Seek wisdom
- ❖ Show forgiveness
- ❖ Make time to worship Christ
- ❖ Don't work (or give gifts) and expect something in return
- ❖ Stifle hidden motives when giving gifts. (In other words, don't buy a gift because you are going to get something in return)
- ❖ Love others without condition

If I find myself working for man instead of God, or if I'm being grumbly about having to do a certain chore (maybe because I'm too tired, or the chore seems redundant or too big) I think of the chore not as something I *have* to do, but something I *get* to do.

So instead of saying, "I *have* to go fold this load of laundry," try saying, "I *get* to fold this load of laundry." It will not only make you feel better, because you are taking the godly approach and being thankful, but you'll also be amazed at what it does to you psychologically!

Let's make it a daily practice to work on these things and endeavor to serve Christ with our whole heart.

Let's not do things "good enough" for Christ. Let's do things to the best of our ability.

He deserves our very best.

CLINGING TO HIS PROMISES

*hat has the Lord promised us?* If I asked you that question, you might be able to come up with a few things.

He'll never leave us, nor forsake us, or, *He'll never flood the earth again,* are a couple of promises that many people remember right off.

But what else has the Lord promised us?

According to one man's count, there are over 5,000 of them recorded in the Bible!

And guess what?

God has kept every single one.

We, as humans, have a hard time keeping just the simple promises of life, yet Christ has kept thousands of them!

We could fill this entire book with the promises of God, and still have room for more. So, for the sake of space, I'm only going to list a few.

Some of these promises, however, are conditional upon the obedience of us, as Christians and servants of Christ.

As you read them, try to think of a way the Lord has already fulfilled this promise in your life (if applicable).

A FEW OF GOD'S PROMISES:

- ❖ **He will give us a new heart** (Ezekiel 26:36)
- ❖ **He gives us His Spirit (to cause us to walk in His ways)** (Ezekiel 36: 27)
- ❖ **He will never leave nor forsake us** (Deuteronomy 31:6)
- ❖ **He forgives us unconditionally** (1 John 1:9)
- ❖ **He rewards those who diligently seek Him** (Hebrews 11:6)

- ❖ Perfect peace (when we trust in Him) (Isaiah 26:3)
- ❖ Everlasting life (John 3:16)
- ❖ If we search for Him, we will find Him (Deuteronomy 4:29)
- ❖ He will protect us (Psalm 121)
- ❖ His love will never fail (1 Chronicles 16:34)
- ❖ He will bless those who delight themselves in His Word (Psalm 1:1-3)
- ❖ Salvation for those who believe (Romans 1:16-17)
- ❖ All things are done for our good (Romans 8:28)
- ❖ Comfort in our trials (2 Corinthians 1:3-4)
- ❖ New life in Christ (2 Corinthians 5:17)
- ❖ Every spiritual blessing (Ephesians 1:3)
- ❖ He will finish the work He started in us (Philippians 1:6)
- ❖ Peace, when we pray (Philippians 4:6-7)
- ❖ God will supply all our needs (Matthew 6:33; Philippians 4:19)

- ❖ **Abundant life (for those who follow Him)** (John 10:10)
- ❖ **Eternal life** (John 4:14)
- ❖ **Nothing can take away our salvation** (John 10:28)
- ❖ **He will return for us** (John 14:2-3)

How precious it is to know that no matter what, God will keep every promise He has made!

He alone will protect us, provide for us, and give us the ultimate gift, *eternal life*.

When should we dwell on God's promises?

All the time!

It's especially helpful to remember them in times of trouble, depression, discouragement, and trials.

God gives us trials to strengthen us, and make us more like Him.

During trials, we often wonder if God's even there. Is He even hearing our prayers? He might seem distant and unavailable, which is where His promise in

Deuteronomy comes to mind: *He will never leave us nor forsake us.*

No matter the time, trial or circumstance, the Lord is always with us, every second of every day.

Call out to Him, and He will answer.

And remember...

Hold to His promises, and never let go.

THE REFLECTION
OF OUR LIVES

The other day, we happened to drive past a sign I'd never noticed before.

After inquiring about it, I was informed that it'd been there for several years.

Yeah, that figures. I've lived here for pretty much all my life, and just now noticed it.

It's the things right in front of us we tend to notice the least, right?

The sign was encouraging residents to "Adopt a Mile" to keep the place free of litter.

The sign was set in a place that looked like it could be the county junkyard.

There was trash for a solid twenty feet on one side of the road.

Everything from a leftover Happy Meal® (the kid's toy was even there, still wrapped) to glass bottles. You name it, and it was probably among the sea of trash.

But after several feet of discarded rubbish, I came upon about ten feet of spotless grass. There wasn't a single bit of garbage in sight.

The clean stretch of earth stuck out like a sore thumb, because it looked so different compared to everything around it.

And then a question came to mind.

Do our lives look any different?

We live in a world where trash (both figurative and literal) are all around us.

Do we blend in with the trash around us?

Or are we like that spotless stretch of earth?

Do our lives reflect the trash of the world?

Or do they reflect the spotlessness of Christ?

Our lives as Christians should reflect Christ, not the filth of this world.

When other people look at you, what do they see?

Are our lives so different from the world that people notice right away that something is different?

I noticed at once that something was different about that spotless stretch of earth.

I noticed that even though it was surrounded by the filthy trash, it still stayed spotless and clean.

There's a scripture in Romans that says:

"Do not conform to the pattern of this world, but be transformed by the renewing of your mind. Then you will be able to test and approve what God's will is—his good, pleasing and perfect will."
ROMANS 12:2

God knew from the beginning of the world that we would live in the midst of evil and pollution.

This was His plan, so that we, as Christians could be lights in the world.

But if our lives are conformed to the world, how then can we be lights?

To be a light for Christ we must be *different.*

We must be in the world, but not of it.

How do we do that?

Here are a few ways:

❖ **Dress modestly**

"Your beauty should not come from outward adornment, such as elaborate hairstyles and the wearing of gold jewelry or fine clothes. Rather, it should be that of your inner self, the unfading beauty of a gentle and quiet spirit, which is of great worth in God's sight."

1 PETER 3:3-4

Some people take that verse and say it's wrong to wear jewelry. I don't think that's what Timothy meant at all. The women in the Bible were all about wearing jewelry. Some of them could even be dubbed as the biggest jewelry wearers of the century. That's probably what prompted Timothy to remind them that jewelry and the outward appearance is not important, but rather the inward appearance of the heart.

❖ Watch what you say

"Nor should there be obscenity, foolish talk or coarse joking, which are out of place, but rather thanksgiving."
EPHESIANS 5:4

You could take this scripture very literally and refuse to speak anything that is remotely sarcastic or even funny, lumping all that into the category of "foolish jesting."

Or, you could take it and commit not only to keep from slandering others (which is a given) but also to put away slang words like, *cool,* or *yeah,* (in the place of yes, ma'am, and yes, sir), and phrases like *"oh my gosh,"* or *"oh my word."*

❖ Latest Fads

"Do not conform to the pattern of this world, but be transformed by the renewing of your mind. Then you will be able to test and approve what God's will is—His good, pleasing and perfect will."
ROMANS 12:2

Don't be concerned about the latest fads in the world. Clothing, jewelry, adapting to the latest texting abbreviations, following all the TV shows that are "in." Being on every social media site; I don't have anything against social media sites, *especially* if they are used for business/ministry. I *do* think we can get sucked into the world of social media quite easily, and especially so if we have an account with every site available, making it very easy to waste the valuable time the Lord has given us.

We can way too easily spend too much time in front of the mirror, obsessing over an appearance that isn't as important as the appearance of our hearts.

Feminism and being *proudly* single are two lifestyles the world has embraced. Though these lifestyles have been around for a while now and definitely aren't recent fads, it's best to stay away from those areas of thinking.

❖ Teach your children diligently

"These commandments that I give you to-day are to be on your hearts. Impress them on your children. Talk about them when you sit at home and when you walk along the road, when you lie down and when you get up."
DEUTERONOMY 6:6-7

Take every situation and turn it into a teaching opportunity. I know a certain missionary who does this with even the smallest things! He was visiting us one time a few years ago, when one of my little siblings started telling him about how their hamster died. This missionary then began reminding us about how short life was, (for both humans *and* animals) and that we should take every opportunity to serve the Lord while we are still living. He took even something as trivial as the death of a hamster and turned it into a teaching opportunity.

❖ Our thoughts

"Finally, brothers and sisters, whatever is true, whatever is noble, whatever is right, whatever is pure, whatever is lovely, whatever is admirable—if anything is excellent or praiseworthy—think about such things."
PHILIPPIANS 4:8

Meditate on heavenly things. We shouldn't always be thinking about the next fun adventure in life, or what we *could* be doing instead of what we *are* doing. We must try our best not to dwell on all the evil in the world, but rather on what is pure and lovely. And remember this: *whatever we put into our minds will come out through our thoughts, words, and actions.*

❖ Debts

"Keep your lives free from the love of money and be content with what you have, because God has said, "Never will I leave you; never will I forsake you."
HEBREWS 13:5

In our day and age, it's hard to be content with what we have. We're always wanting more and more, never being satisfied with enough. We want what we can't have. We want what our friends have. We desire sinful things. And a lot of times, we get what we want. Why? Because we go in debt. We borrow money to buy things we don't have the money for, and most times we don't even need the item.

We need to try to keep from taking out loans on houses, cars, and other big items. We should save up our money until we can buy the item and then pay cash for it. What was it "Pa" on *Little House on the Prairie* always said? "Cash on the barrel" (meaning immediate payment). If we are in debt, we should endeavor to get out of it. If you are striving to be debt free, I greatly encourage you to keep striving! Every sacrifice will be worth it in the end. If you are debt free, then you are familiar with that feeling of freedom and relief it gives you to not be under the clutches of debt.

Even small debts, such as owing your parents or siblings money. When my parents started *really* trying to pay off the mortgage on our house, they included all of us in that endeavor. My Daddy made a chart and every few weeks we'd get to color a few blocks until we reached that top goal. For a while, we all felt the clutches of debt as we pinched pennies to put *all* we could into the mortgage fund. And then when we paid it off? We *all* felt the relief of actually being debt free! And I must say, even though I wasn't even the one paying off the debt, the excitement and lighthearted feeling of our parents was contagious enough for us all to share of that joy.

❖ Movies

"I will not look with approval on anything that is vile. I hate what faithless people do; I will have no part in it."
PSALM 101:3

I first want to start off by saying that not all movies are bad. *But*, if we gathered all the movies together (especially the newly released ones) and put them into categories of good or bad, the bad would definitely outweigh the good. Because of that, we must be so very careful of what we set before our eyes. There's a scene in one of my favorite movies, *Time Changer,* where the main character comes running out of the theater yelling, "Stop the movie! Stop the movie! They just blasphemed the name of the Lord our God!"

You see, that's the furthest reaction we see from people (and even some Christians) nowadays. They are desensitized and unbothered by it. But we should be offended and upset when we hear someone blaspheme our Father's name.

And remember: it only takes one second for an image or word to flash across the screen and imbed itself in our minds.

❖ Music

"So whether you eat or drink or whatever you do, do it all for the glory of God."
I CORINTHIANS 10:31

There are some sinfully polluted songs and music genres in the world. The words and the style are the farthest thing from "Christian," and don't bring glory to God's name in any way. I don't listen to rock music. I would never tell you that it's sinful to listen to rock music. I know of some rock bands who are Christians, and I would never (and can't) judge a heart. But, I don't think we should make it a practice to listen to this genre. Don't you think it would be much better to listen to hymns and other spiritual songs? *(Ephesians 5:19)*

A lot of songs nowadays have continuous repeating, (even Christian songs). It's as if they are trying to hypnotize you, (and some churches have music bands that do just that!). How much better would it be if we sang songs like, Be Thou My Vision, or Nearer My God to Thee? Let's try our best to put only God honoring music into our minds.

The world is changing all around us; but that doesn't mean we must change with it. In fact, if we don't "go with the flow" of the world and conform ourselves with them, then the world will be sure to notice that something is different. It may prompt someone to ask us *why* we are different. If we are ever confronted with that question, we must be ready to give an answer (1 Peter 3:15).

And remember this...

"Where your mind dwells, your heart is sure to follow."

I'LL GO
WITH YOU

"Once upon a time—it was back in the days when judges led Israel—there was a famine in the land. A man from Bethlehem in Judah left home to live in the country of Moab, he and his wife and his two sons. The man's name was Elimelech; his wife's name was Naomi; his sons were named Mahlon and Kilion—all Ephrathites from Bethlehem in Judah. They all went to the country of Moab and settled there.

Elimelech died and Naomi was left, she and her two sons. The sons took Moabite wives; the name of the first was Orpah, the second Ruth. They lived there in Moab *for the next ten years. But then the two brothers, Mahlon and Kilion, died. Now the woman was left without either her young men or her husband.*

One day she got herself together, she and her two daughters-in-law, to leave the country of Moab and set out for home; she had heard that God had been pleased to visit his people and give them food. And so she started out from the place she had been living, she and her two daughters-in-law with her, on the road back to the land of Judah.

After a short while on the road, Naomi told her two daughters-in-law, "Go back. Go home and live with your mothers. And may God treat you as graciously as you treated your deceased husbands and me. May God give each of you a new home and a new husband!" She kissed them and they cried openly.

They said, "No, we're going on with you to your people."

But Naomi was firm: "Go back, my dear daughters. Why would you come with me? Do you suppose I still have sons in my womb who can become your future husbands? Go back, dear daughters—on your way, please! I'm too old to get a husband. Why, even if I said, 'There's still hope!' and this very night got a man and had sons, can you imagine being satisfied to wait until they were grown? Would you wait that long to get married again? No, dear daughters; this is a bitter pill for me to swallow—more bitter for me than for you. God has dealt me a hard blow."

Again they cried openly. Orpah kissed her mother-in-law good-bye; but Ruth embraced her and held on.

Naomi said, "Look, your sister-in-law is going back home to live with her own people and gods; go with her."

But Ruth said, "Don't force me to leave you; don't make me go home. Where you go, I go; and where you live, I'll live. Your people are my people, your God is my God; where you die, I'll die, and that's where I'll be buried, so help me God—not even death itself is going to come between us!"

When Naomi saw that Ruth had her heart set on going with her, she gave in. And so the two of them traveled on together to Bethlehem" (Ruth 1:1-17 MSG).

What were Ruth's words to Naomi?

"Don't force me to leave you; don't make me go home. Where you go, I go; and where you live, I'll live. Your people are my people, your God is my God; where you die, I'll die, and that's where I'll be buried, so help me God—not even death itself is going to come between us!"

Shouldn't we have this same attitude towards Christ and His people?

Shouldn't we be saying: *"Don't force me to leave You, Lord. I'll go where You lead me, and live where You put me. I want to be with Your people. Not even death itself can separate me from Your Love!"*

Ruth had unconditionally given herself to Naomi. So much so, that she cared nothing about her own desires, and definitely not of her safety and wellbeing.

She was a Moabite woman, and in Bethlehem she would be looked down upon, to say the least.

But she forsook all her own feelings and gave everything she had to Naomi.

Her love.

Her trust.

Everything.

And she trusted that God alone would keep her safe.

As Christians, we should be ready to say, "Don't leave me or forsake me, Lord!"

Or as the Psalmist said many times, "Don't turn your face away from me."

What parallels can we find in our life, with the words Ruth spoke to Naomi?

❖ **We should be content to stay where God puts us.**

"Therefore I tell you, do not worry about your life, what you will eat or drink; or about your body, what you will wear. Is not life more than food, and the body

more than clothes? Look at the birds of the air; they do not sow or reap or store away in barns, and yet your heavenly Father feeds them. Are you not much more valuable than they?"
MATTHEW 6:25-26

We should be happy and content wherever the Lord has us.

Whether it's in a house that we think is too small or a car we don't think is nice enough. Living with rowdy kids, or with a person who's hard to get along with. Wherever He puts us, He puts us there for a reason and a purpose, so shouldn't we show our thanks by being content?

We should be ready to go where He leads us, without looking back. If the Lord were to tell us to pack up our houses and move to another country, would we go willingly? Or would we look back at what we were leaving behind? If the Lord tells us to do something or to go somewhere, we should obey Him without looking back. And keep in mind what happened to a certain woman who looked back instead of trusting God and moving forward (Genesis 19:26). The Bible says she became a "pillar of salt." Dead. Unmovable. Lifeless. Why? Because instead of trusting God, and caring more about Him than the riches of this world, she looked back.

❖ **We should desire to be with God's people and to fellowship with other believers.**

"...Instead, be filled with the Spirit, speaking to one another with psalms, hymns, and songs from the Spirit. Sing and make music from your heart to the Lord."
EPHESIANS 5:18-19

"Therefore encourage one another and build each other up, just as in fact you are doing."
1 THESSALONIANS 5:11

As Christians, we should desire to be with other like-minded believers. If we call ourselves Christians, yet don't yearn for the fellowship of other sisters and brothers in Christ, there's something big missing in our lives. And as my daddy says, "Failure to love the church (the body of Christ) is a failure to love Christ."

And the fellowshipping of believers doesn't only encourage each member, but it strengthens, refreshes and proves to be a continuous accountability.

❖ **Nothing can separate us from God's love.**

"For I am convinced that neither death nor life, neither angels nor demons, neither the present nor the future, nor any powers, neither height nor depth, nor anything else in all creation, will be able to separate us from the love of God that is in Christ Jesus our Lord."
ROMANS 8:38-39

Absolutely nothing can separate us from the love of God!

Nothing. Nada. Zilch.

Not. One. Thing.

God's love is so powerful and so mighty. It's everlasting and unconditional. And if we are children of God, nothing can ever take away that love.

In C.H. Spurgeon's sermon, *More Than Conquers,* he says: *"Most conquerors have to struggle and agonize to win the conquest, but Christians, when their love to Christ is strong, have found it even easy to overcome suffering for the Lord."*

Spurgeon described that perfectly! Because of Christ's love, every day trials can be turned into blessings and our mourning into dancing. (Psalm 30:11)

Because of Christ's love we have the strength and encouragement to journey on day to day. And His love, as the hymn *The Love of God,* describes it, is greater than tongue can tell. It's immeasurable, it's priceless, and it's shown towards who?

Us.

And nothing, absolutely nothing, can ever take it away.

THE LOVE OF GOD

The love of God is greater far
Than tongue or pen can ever tell
It goes beyond the highest star
And reaches to the lowest hell
The guilty pair, bowed down with care
God gave His Son to win
His erring child He reconciled
And pardoned from his sin

Could we with ink the ocean fill
And were the skies of parchment made
Were every stalk on earth a quill
And every man a scribe by trade

To write the love of God above
Would drain the ocean dry
Nor could the scroll contain the whole
Though stretched from sky to sky

O love of God, how rich and pure!
How measureless and strong!
It shall forevermore endure
The saints' and angels' song

NO FEAR
IN DEATH

There's a certain assisted living home we go to regularly. We love visiting with them, and playing gospel bluegrass music for the residents.

Our purpose is to glorify God and bless the residents there, but what ends up happening more often than naught, is that we are the ones feeling blessed.

We're blessed by the smiles and faces of pure delight by the dear ladies and gentlemen.

We're blessed by the way their eyes sparkle when they tell us, "you made my day special," "this is my favorite day every month!" and "God has really blessed your family, hasn't He?"

We're blessed, because we see how God has taken our music, and miraculously turned it into something that could bless another's heart.

Each resident has their own unique personality.

Each one has their own smile, their own way of enjoying the music, and their own way of participating in the program.

But one certain resident seems to have been born with a double dose.

This dear lady never forgets to playfully remind us that we are all her grandchildren (or children, it changes periodically) and that she loves us all very much.

She smiles during every song. She sings along (as do most of the residents) faithfully. And she can almost always be seen with her camera, taking pictures.

She's even been known to get them developed and brings us copies from time to time!

Her memory is astounding, and she even asks about our grandparents, (who have visited only once, and live ten hours away!)

I had the pleasure of speaking with her during one of our visits a couple of days ago.

It was then I began to fully understand the hand of cards life had dealt her, and how faithfully she had played each one.

She had a daughter who grew sick when she was about fifteen years old.

They knew something was very wrong, but all the doctors would ever say was, "she's fine."

They knew that wasn't the truth, and they told the doctors so, but they wouldn't admit her to the hospital, and since they didn't know what else to do, they took their daughter home.

Through a series of phone calls, and prayers later, they were finally about to bring their daughter back to the hospital, in hopes that this time they would be given an answer concerning the state of her health.

But it was too late.

It was early one morning when the fifteen-year-old girl stared out the hospital window into the darkness of the morning and asked her mother, "Mama, what time is it?"

Her mother told her, but then asked, "Why do you want to know what time it is?"

Her daughter answered, "Because I'm going to die. And I don't want to die in the darkness, but when it's light I'll be ready to go."

And when the sun rose above the mountain and peeked into the window of that tiny hospital room, her daughter went to be with the Lord.

This young girl didn't fear death. She didn't grow anxious about dying and leaving her earthly home.

I didn't have the pleasure of meeting this young girl, but according to her mother she was a devoted Christian.

She didn't fear dying. Her only desire was that she die in the *light.*

We've already covered the topic of being lights in the midst of darkness.

We've discussed what it means to be *a light for Christ,* and we've dwelt on what it looks like when we are being true lights.

But once our time on this earth has expired, once our purpose in this life is complete, once we've lived our lives according to Christ's will...then what?

Death is not something many of us like to dwell on.

As I've heard various people say, "It's not being dead that troubles me, it's the *dying* part."

Have you felt the same way before? Do you feel that way now?

Fearing death is a fear that many of us have. It's a fear that I myself have had to confront before.

During my searching, I've found things that have blessed and encouraged me greatly.

This is what I discovered: For starters, (as we've already covered) fear is most often times wrong, and sinful. Very few fears are good fears to have.

We are told in the scriptures over and over again to, *fear not.* And why? Because Christ is with us.

C.H. Spurgeon says: *"The fear of death is natural to man as a sinner."*

But he also says: *"While the fear of death is natural to the sinner, it is not necessary to the saint."*

Though fearing death isn't a necessary fear for Christians, and by the grace of God some of us have been delivered from it. It is still a very real fear in many of our lives.

C.H. Spurgeon says in his sermon, *The Fear of Death,* that death can be our best friend! *"Beloved brothers and sisters in Christ, there is no need that you should be afraid to die! It is even possible for you to look upon death as your best friend! You may yet come to be familiar with the shroud, the mattock, the grave—and find the cemetery to be no place of gloom and may even rejoice in the prospect of death."*

Even though we think we may have a reason to fear death, all our reasons can be contradicted with God's Word. Here are just a few of the scriptures that deal with fearing death:

"Do not let your hearts be troubled. You believe in God; believe also in me. My Father's house has many rooms; if that were not so, would I have told you that I am going there to prepare a place for you? And if I go and prepare a place for you, I will come back and take you to be with me that you also may be where I am. You know the way to the place where I am going."
JOHN 14:1-4

"Since the children have flesh and blood, he too shared in their humanity so that by his death he might break the power of him who holds the power of death—that is, the devil—and free those who all their lives were held in slavery by their fear of death."
HEBREWS 2:14-15

"Yea, though I walk through the valley of
the shadow of death, I will fear no evil:
for thou art with me; thy rod and thy staff
they comfort me."
PSALM 23:4 KJV

"Therefore, we are always confident
and know that as long as we are at home
in the body we are away from the Lord.
For we live by faith, not by sight. We
are confident, I say, and would prefer
to be away from the body and at home
with the Lord."
2 CORINTHIANS 5:6-8

"For to me, to live is Christ
and to die is gain."
PHILIPPIANS 1:21

C.H Spurgeon says at the closing of
his sermon: *"It may not be long before
some of us will have our faith tested in our
dying hour. The preacher may be called
away or you may receive the summons first.
It would be well if we were all so familiar*

with death that we could say as one old saint did, "Dying? Why, I have died daily for the last 20 years, so I am not afraid to die, now!" Or, as another said, "I dip my foot in Jordan's stream every morning before I take my breakfast, so I shall not be afraid to go down into the stream whenever my Lord bids me enter it." May that be your experience and mine, Beloved, and then we shall have no fear of death!"

Let us endeavor to fear nothing! Not even death itself.

As you've just read, when we are absent from the body we are present with the Lord!

And how precious it is to be reminded that when we pass on, we will live with Christ in Heaven for eternity!

Do you have the blessed assurance and peace that your name is written in the Book of Life? Do you know without a doubt that when you die, you will be in Heaven with the Lord?

If not, take the time to search the depths of your heart and confront the lingering doubt in your mind.

As the scripture says, *"And as it is appointed unto men once to die, but after this the judgment"* (Hebrews 9:27 KJV).

Pray to the Lord and ask Him to free you from the bondage of sin. Ask Him to forgive you of all your transgressions. Endeavor to live your life according to His will.

I once heard a missionary friend say: "We will either be on fire for Christ in this world, or in the lake of fire in torment for eternity."

Strive to please the Lord and follow His example.

We, as Christians don't have to fear death. There's nothing to fear! Why? Because, "Death is no punishment to the believer: it is the gate of endless joy" (C.H. Spurgeon).

NO FEAR OF DEATH

No fear of death, so shall it be,
When deaths tight grasp has hold of me.
No sigh of fear, no tears of doubt,
No wavering of my faith about.
Just perfect peace in my Savior I will lay,
My trust in Him shall forever stay.
For when death's final curse has won,
I then will see the Father and His beloved Son.
Into my Father's arms I'll run,
And say, "Not mine, but His will was done."

THE
MIRROR

ith your eyes half-shut, you turn over and hit the snooze button on your alarm clock. A few minutes later, you roll out of bed and stumble your way to the bathroom.

You stand in front of the mirror and glance into its revealing depths.

You're somewhat frightened at what stares back at you.

Your hair is a mess.

Your face needs a good washing.

And you're positively sure that your teeth most definitely need brushed.

Your trusty mirror revealed all this to you.

But can the mirror fix your appearance?

It showed you your imperfections, but it can't fix them.

God's law does this exact same thing. The Ten Commandments are a tool in showing us our sin.

They're like that mirror. But just like the mirror, the law can't fix our sin.

"Anyone who listens to the word but does not do what it says is like someone who looks at his face in a mirror and, after looking at himself, goes away and immediately forgets what he looks like. But whoever looks intently into the perfect law that gives freedom, and continues in it—not forgetting what they have heard, but doing it—they will be blessed in what they do."
JAMES 1:23-25

Let us not be like that man who looks into the mirror and goes away, not caring to change his appearance.

The only time we see our outward appearance is when we look into the mirror. It's the world (and God) who sees us the rest of the time.

When the world looks at us, the most they can see is the outward appearance. They can't see into our mind and heart.

But God can.

When God looks into our hearts, what does He see?

Are you comfortable with what He finds there?

It's important that we guard our hearts and minds from the sins and lusts of this world. But how do we do that?

We must constantly pray the words as David did, *"Create in me a pure heart, O God and renew a steadfast spirit within me"* (Psalm 51:10).

We must guard our hearts against the immorality of this world.

How do we clean our hearts and minds? How do we constantly make sure our thoughts and meditations are pure and holy in His sight?

❖ Get spiritually healthy

"Let us draw near to God with a sincere heart and with the full assurance that faith brings, having our hearts sprinkled to cleanse us from a guilty conscience and having our bodies washed with pure water."
HEBREWS 10:22

We can't clean ourselves. But God can. We must draw near to God and ask Him to help clean the areas of our lives that need cleaning. We must wash ourselves with the Word and be constantly committing scriptures to memory.

❖ Clean your mouth

"A good man brings good things out of the good stored up in his heart, and an evil man brings evil things out of the evil stored up in his heart. For the mouth speaks what the heart is full of."
LUKE 6:45

As our hearts are being cleaned, so should our mouths. How many times do we get corrected (by a parent, or God) concerning the words of our mouth? Blasphemy, negativity, complaining; put away all these things.

Do you have a hard time with a certain individual? Commit to saying one kind thing about them today.

❖ Repent from hidden sins

"When I kept silent,
my bones wasted away
through my groaning all day long.
For day and night
your hand was heavy on me;
my strength was sapped
as in the heat of summer.
Then I acknowledged my sin to you
and did not cover up my iniquity.
I said, "I will confess my transgressions to the Lord."
And you forgave
the guilt of my sin."
PSALM 32:3-5

We've all experienced at one time or another, the heavy weight of a burdened conscience. We know the grief it causes, the heartache it brings. But even more than that, we know the feeling of weightlessness, the feeling of joy and happiness, when that burden is confessed, and lifted from our shoulders.

If we have a hidden sin in our lives, we must first acknowledge that we can't hide it from God, and then be quick to bring it to Him. We must humble ourselves enough to make a confession to those around us (James 5:16) if our sin has hurt them in any way.

This is one of the most important steps in having a clean heart. We must keep nothing "hidden" from our Father, parents, spouses, children, or siblings. We need to cleanse our conscience and give our burdens to Him. He will bless us for it.

❖ **Don't harbor unforgiveness and bitterness**

"Get rid of all bitterness, rage and anger, brawling and slander, along with every form of malice. Be kind and compassionate to one another, forgiving each other, just as in Christ God forgave you."
EPHESIANS 4:31-32

Any sin is a burden, but the sin of unforgiveness and bitterness is so confining, we might not even know it's there. We've had it for so long, we've just accepted it as a part of our lives, not even noticing that it's been slowly eating away at our joy and happiness. Need I tell you not to keep bitterness and unforgiveness close to your heart? If we find ourselves harboring these feelings towards someone, we must take it to the Lord and entreat Him to cleanse away those sinful feelings.

❖ **Remember that Jesus is a part of every day**

"God is faithful, who has called you
into fellowship with his Son, Jesus
Christ our Lord."
1 CORINTHIANS 1:9

"For you have delivered me from death
and my feet from stumbling, that I may
walk before God in the light of life."
PSALM 56:13

Did you wake up this morning? Did you eat breakfast? Were you able to walk around the house on two strong feet and use your own arms to get yourself ready for the day? Each of these things (and so many more) are things we often take for granted. The only reason we woke up this morning was because of *Jesus.* The only reason we were able to eat breakfast and walk around and use our arms and hands, is because of *Jesus.* The only reason we are able to draw our very next breath is because the Lord has shown mercy upon us. So why not acknowledge His presence and make Him a part of our daily lives? Do we pray before each meal? Are we quick to pray and thank Him when things turn out in our favor (or when they don't)?

Are we religiously studying the Words He has given us, and committing them to our hearts? If not, He wants to help us do these things. We are His children. He wants our all. We must be ready to give up everything for Christ and show Him even in the littlest ways that we love Him and appreciate what He has done in our lives.

Let's endeavor to use the law correctly. It's impossible to follow the Ten Commandments perfectly, but its purpose isn't to be followed anyway.

Its purpose is to show us our sin.

Let's do our best to look into the mirror the Lord has given us. Let us not be calloused and ignore the filth we see when we see our reflection.

When we look into the mirror in the morning and see a blemish on our face, we are quick to fix it the best way we know how.

Let's do the same thing when we see the blemishes of our heart.

And remember, the mirror of the law doesn't have the power to cleanse our sin.

That's why Jesus has offered to fix us, clean us, and take our burdens upon Himself (Matthew 11:29-30).

Let's take Him up on His offer, shall we? He is much more capable in dealing with our burdens.

Let's be willing to take everything to Him and be humble students of our King.

ALEIGHA C. ISRAEL, writer of inspirational fiction and poetry, is an author of six books and enjoys sharing God's love through the powerful art of storytelling.

Her novels are distributed by Grace and Truth Books and have been enjoyed by ages nine to ninety-three!

With two amazing parents and five of the greatest siblings, there's always another adventure just waiting around the corner!

To learn more about Aleigha and to sign up for her weekly blog post, visit: www.thepenofthewriter.weebly.com

Also by Aleigha C. Israel

INSPIRATIONAL FICTION

 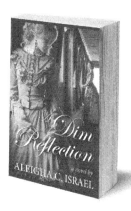

POETRY

A Higher Ransom : Book 1

A thrilling tale from start to finish!

Two lives so vastly different from each other... are about to be given a choice that will change the course of their lives forever. King Raymond is ruthless. He will stop at nothing to see that every Christian is diminished. But Anna Haddington doesn't understand why she must keep quiet about her faith. When her plans to stay with her aunt in Carpathia go quickly awry, Anna finds it takes all that is in her to trust God with the outcome. This is a story full of mystery and sacrifice that will leave you questioning whether you have what it takes to give up everything for Christ, even your very own life. Discover the account of three lives, all so different from each other. And find out how one person's decision can affect the lives of so many. Will Anna stand strong and not waver in her faith? Or will she crumble under the rule of the heartless king?

A LIGHT FOR CHRIST
COLLECTION

A Dim Reflection : Book 2

A sequel that will touch your heart!

William Caverly can't seem to understand the unsettling feeling that has been nagging him for far too long. Memories of a baby sister are forever haunting his waking hours, and as he sleeps at night, he is repeatedly awakened by nightmares, confusing ones that he'd rather forget. He had been told that his baby sister died. He had seen her little body laid to rest beside their mother. But that didn't explain the dim remembrance that he had of an event that happened not too long after that. Charlotte Porter's days are full and busy as she diligently teaches her young art students at her mother's boarding school, and tries desperately to stay away from an annoying suitor. Painting has been her passion and dream ever since she could hold a brush, but lately she has begun to question her mission and calling in life. What is her real purpose? And why does she know so little about her father, who supposedly died before she was born? William thinks he's discovered the hidden link that has kept him from his sister for over fifteen years. But then she's kid-napped, leaving William no choice except to find her and get her back. Once and for all.

Poetry Books

by Aleigha C. Israel

A beautiful array of poems about Love, Friendship, God, and so much more! These books are filled with adorable illustrations drawn by Aleigha's family that are sure to make you smile. Also included is information about how to easily memorize God's Word!

The Pen of the Writer
— online

thepenofthewriter.weebly.com

Stay informed about my books, sales, giveaways and more!

Sign up for my newsletter featuring short devotionals, guest posts, and spotlighting some of my favorite Christian authors.

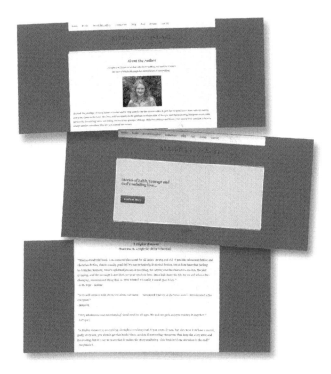

Your support means everything to me!
Thank you!

ADVERTISEMENTS

Following a trail of archeological discoveries from Gensis to Jesus

A growing number of people today think the Bible is filled with fairy tales and fables, but the author contends there are literally thousands of discoveries from archaeology that support the Bible as historically accurate and reliable. In this informative yet easy-to-read book, Jan Sessions shares her personal "journey of enlightenment," including many faith building discoveries from her own research as well as eye-witness observations from her recent trip to Israel and Jordan. Fables Don't Leave Footprints contains over 120 full-color photographs of what the author calls "footprints"—physical, outside-the-Bible evidences left behind by people, places, and events recorded in the Bible. Based on the evidence, there are more reasons than ever to believe!

Jan Session, Author

Doula View
helping new parents every day

You hire a broker to help you navigate through the process of buying a house. You hire a lawyer to help guide you through dealing with insurance claims. You hire a wedding planner to help plan and organize your wedding. Why would you not want an advocate to help you navigate through one of the most amazing, but stressful, experiences of your life?

A doula is a highly trained non-medical birth professional. Her job is to provide you with information and advice so that you can make informed decisions throughout the birth process. In addition, a lot of expectant parents can feel rushed and bullied by medical staff into making decisions that may not be right for their family. A doula can offer support by being a buffer between you and medical staff and help you to take a breath so you can make the right decisions for you.

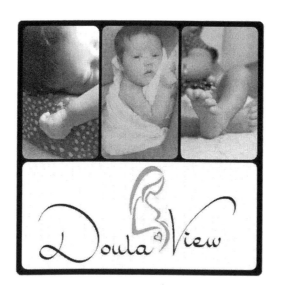

Call for your free consultation!

CONTACT INFO:

 770-882-4544

latoya@lamazedoula.com

www.lamazedoula.com

The call to be the Hands and Feet of Jesus in the midst of Injustice.

There are more slaves today than any other time in history, babies are being brutally murdered in their mother's womb, orphans are left alone and uncared for, human life is disregarded, and souls are dying without knowing Jesus. This is something many of us don't know, or know but don't really think about, or think about, but don't really do anything about. But God is calling us to do justly, love mercy, and walk humbly, not in our own strength, but in His. In this book, you'll find information about the injustices, inspiration to take action, real-life stories of people, past and present, who answered God's call upon their lives, and a list of 102 ways you can take action, starting today. No matter how unqualified you may feel, God will use you to bring justice in this dark and broken world.

About the Author

Savannah Jane McCrary is an aspiring writer, homeschool student, and, above all, a daughter of the King of Kings. She's the third of seven siblings and loves her family, singing and playing the harp, reading, drawing, photography, history, and cups of hot tea. Her passion is to follow Jesus wholeheartedly and encourage others to do the same.

www.writtenonyourheart.weebly.com

Ivory Roses Pianist

Weddings, parties, formal dinners, etc.

Every event is better with music!

CONTACT HANNAH MICHELLE:

404-368-0610

ivoryrosespianist@gmail.com

ivoryrosespianist.wixsite.com/mysite

Heritage Arrows

Embroidery & Design

We are a family owned and operated business that provides quality embroidered products. We offer customized digitizing, embroidered shirts and caps, monograms, and more!

CONTACT INFO:

573-766-8021

heritagearrows16@gmail.com

Heritage Arrows
Embroidery & Design

The perfect keepsake for your loved ones!

Che Designs

Are you looking for a special gift for a special occasion? Or maybe a special gift for a special person? Che Designs specializes in making personalized, beautiful gifts for every occasion! Weddings, birthdays, baby showers, graduation, or "just because."

Everything from baskets, pillow cases, and blankets, Che Designs will work to ensure you have the *perfect* gift for your occasion!

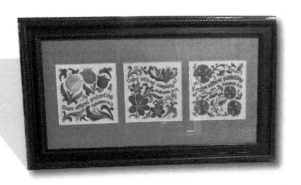

CONTACT INFO:

 678-794-5246

cherrylsullivan49@gmail.com

Che Designs
Always the perfect gift!

integrity & innovation

I work one on one with self-publishing authors and musicians, designing covers, layouts, merchandise, ads, websites, etc.

CONTACT INFO:

501-242-3879

o.m.faye@aol.com

Thank you for reading!

God bless you!

Made in the USA
Columbia, SC
21 August 2017